Ahas!

Moments of inspired thought

Many of the designations used by manufacturers and sellers to distinguish their products are claimed as trademarks. Where those designations appear in this book and Aspen Light Publishing was aware of a trademark claim, those designations have been printed with initial capital letters.

Copyright © 2016 by John P. Strelecky

All rights reserved. No part of this publication may be reproduced, stored in a retrieval system, or transmitted, in any form or by any means, electronic, mechanical, photocopying, recording, or otherwise, without the prior written permission of the publisher.

Printed in the United States of America.

Publication Data:
Strelecky, John P.
Ahas! / John P. Strelecky. 1st Aspen Light Publishing ed.

ISBN-13: 978-0-991-39209-4

Published by Aspen Light Publishing
Inquiries to the author can be directed to:

John P. Strelecky c/o Aspen Light Publishing
13506 Summerport Village Parkway Suite #155
Windermere, FL 34786
The author can be reached through
www.johnpstrelecky.com

Ahas!

Moments of inspired thought

John P. Strelecky

Aspen Light Publishing

Ahas!

Other Works by John P. Strelecky

The Why Cafe

Return to The Why Cafe

Life Safari

The Big Five for Life

The Big Five for Life - Continued

How to be Rich and Happy (co-author)

The Mommy Butterfly and the Baby Egg (children's book)

Preface

Welcome to the book of Ahas! As you flip through these pages, you'll discover a variety of inspirational moments.

Learnings about life. Learnings about self. Ideas, thoughts, concepts, flashes of insight and inspiration....

All connected by the common thread that they produced an Aha! experience when they were first discovered. Most of the Ahas! are less than a page. A few a bit longer. Each with its own special energy.

This is a wonderfully random book. On a random whim, at a random time, open the book to any random point and begin reading. You are likely to find that what you discover on those pages, is exactly what you need for that moment in your life.

It's a bit of a mystery, really. How the book, your mind, the universe, a higher power...all conspire to make that happen.

Somehow though, it does.

Enjoy!

P.S. As you are reading these pages, new Ahas! of your own are likely to spring forth. The margins make excellent places to write them down. As does the back of the book. Or anywhere else you feel called to use.

Ahas!

It's how I respond when things are tough, or when I'm most afraid, which shows my true character. Taking the high road is easy—when there's no potholes.

Ahas!

There aren't many oranges in a blueberry patch.

When I give myself the freedom to be in the right place, at the right time, with the right people, I dramatically increase my chances of living the life I really want.

I should stop hanging out in blueberry patches if what I really want…is an orange.

Ahas!

Even the smallest amount of light eliminates the oppressive darkness.

Giving myself the freedom to spend even a few minutes doing what I love, changes the energy of my whole day. When I play one of my favorite songs, talk with one of my friends, read a chapter from a book I love...it changes everything.

Ahas!

I remember earlier in life when I was really struggling with my self-confidence, I would often feel jealous of the success of others. I think that's part of what kept success from me for so long.

Because the truth is, jealousy is a wasted emotion. I should celebrate the success of others. Their success proves it is possible. Not just for them, but for me and everyone else too.

They have just charted a path through the jungle. If I want the success they have, I now have a path to follow. Which is a lot easier than having to be the first one who carves the path.

Ahas!

*A*ll anger is a manifestation of fear.

I'm driving. A car comes out of nowhere and almost runs into me. I swerve to the left and slam on my brakes to avoid it. I'm furious. How could the driver be so stupid? Why weren't they paying attention? What an idiot. Probably texting and driving at the same time. How could they be so reckless?

By the time those thoughts have finished running through my mind, the other driver is five cars ahead of me.

I'm safe. I wasn't hit. It's over. But I still feel angry. Why?

The truth is, I'm not angry because the other driver almost hit me. I'm afraid. Afraid because financially, things have been tough for me lately. I'm not sure I have enough money to repair my car if it was badly damaged.

That would mean I wouldn't be able to drive. If I couldn't drive, I'd lose my job. If I lost my job, I wouldn't be able to pay my rent and I'd be kicked out of my apartment. If I didn't have a car, a job, or an apartment, I'd end up alone, hungry, and homeless, living under a bridge.

I'm not angry because they almost hit me. I'm afraid because I don't want to be alone, hungry, and homeless, living under a bridge.

None of which is really likely to happen…even if I was hit.

Ahas!

When I feel myself becoming angry—about anything—I ask myself—"What am I afraid of right now?" I keep working down through the layers of answers until I get to the real answer. Which is almost always a scenario which is very unlikely to become real.

What I learn from asking that question, and through the answers in those layers...puts things in perspective, and sets me free from the anger.

Overnight success happens with about three years worth of dedicated effort.

It seems like people are giving up sooner and sooner on their dreams. They come up with a great idea, or hear of a career that would interest them, or learn about some fascinating place they want to visit.... But then when a day, or week, or month goes by and things haven't materialized, they start thinking it's never going to happen.

The more people I meet who have done really interesting things, created cool companies, visited fascinating places, the more I see a trend—it often takes a while. And it takes dedicated effort.

It's almost like the universe/God/whatever force is driving this whole process, is looking to make sure we are committed to something before it starts to help.

Once we demonstrate the commitment, and make real effort, then things start to happen a lot faster. Without that though, it's like the energy doesn't know where to apply itself, so it does nothing.

Ahas!

The more time I spend in ways that fill my heart, the less time I'm willing to spend in ways that don't.

Ahas!

The mountain looks highest from the bottom.

Time to start walking.

Ahas!

If I'm not careful, most of my perception of "reality" is formed not by myself, but by the actions of a small group of perception makers.

For every "super model" there are a thousand other woman just as pretty. But someone decided to label those super models as the "most" beautiful, or "most sexy". If I'm going to accept labels, at least let them be the ones I apply.

Ahas!

I've always followed the rules. I now realize that isn't so smart. Instead of following all the rules other people have created, it makes more sense to follow the one's I feel are fair and just.

Because the truth is, the rule makers are often the one's who aren't following them. Especially when it comes to their own self interests. They're also the first ones to tell everyone else they should follow the rules.

I can't believe it's taken me almost three decades to realize this.

This doesn't mean I should break rules just for the sake of breaking them. That's stupid, pointless, and likely to get me in stupid and pointless kinds of trouble.

It does mean I should question things and then make my own decisions.

Ahas!

I live the life I am willing to accept. Either I don't push myself to see other options, or I don't take action to live those other options.

Or I have already found my nirvana.

Ahas!

Finding significance in the face of my obvious insignificance is one of the great adventures of being alive. It challenges me. It pushes me. Sometimes it keeps me awake at night.

Why am I here?

How does this whole game work?

What is the point of all this?

Somewhere within the answer to those questions, there is an amazing new perspective on everything around me.

Ahas!

Never stop praising your child. It means just as much when they are six, sixteen, or twenty-six, as it did when they were only six months old.

This applies to pretty much everyone else in life too.

Ahas!

I choose to be happy today.

Making that choice seems to be the difference.

I have reached an authentic state of knowing, when the strength of my belief does not waver based on the percentage of other people who hold the same belief.

This awareness came to me when I was accosted by an overly zealous individual. Although he seemed deeply committed to his beliefs, I think in truth, he is only tenuously holding onto them. Because the minute he realized my beliefs were different from his, it moved him to extreme agitation. He kept trying to convince me to believe what he believed.

When I didn't immediately do that, he became even more agitated. It was as if the presence of alternate beliefs made him deeply question his own. At least on an unconscious level.

Ahas!

I'm going to remember that guy. He'll remind me to love, not fear those moments where I question my beliefs. Because that questioning is what helps me sculpt, mold, and polish my beliefs until they go from a belief to a known. They are what help me grow.

Ahas!

The biggest barrier to my personal growth and happiness is my refusal to take responsibility for what is going on in my life. If I don't like something, then change it. And keep changing it until I do like it.

Ahas!

*B*eer goggles are where I start to see people different than I did before. They get put on after I've had too much alcohol. My impressions when I wear them are mostly false.

Spirit goggles are where I see people different than I did before too. They get put on when I stop judging. I stop evaluating people by the way they dress, the car they drive, the position they hold, or the way they look. Instead, I see them for who they really are inside.

My impressions when I wear spirit goggles are truth. Sometimes for the very first time.

The more time I spend on things I like, the less pointless life feels.

The reverse is also true.

Ahas!

After careful analysis, it appears there are two options for the explanation of my life.

Option #1

My parents had sex. Nine months later I was born. I'll live a life that statistically speaking lasts around 28,900 days. Hopefully more. Possibly less. Statistically speaking, I'll get around 28,900 days. Then I'll die. There is nothing after. There was nothing before. This is it.

Option #2

I was something before I was born. Spirit, energy... something. When I die, I'll go back to being whatever I was before I was born. Spirit, energy...something. This life is not the beginning and the end compressed between an average of 28,900 days. It is a brief stop of a soul who was curious about what it would be like to be human for a while.

Ahas!

Regardless of which one of these options is true, I might as well enjoy life and stop worrying so much.

Ahas!

I can't control the ways others act around me, or treat me. I can always control how I respond. Whether I stay or go is up to me. Whether I take it personally or not, is up to me. Whether I accept their love and return it...is up to me.

Ahas!

Getting to a second great adventure requires taking a step towards a first great adventure. Often that step is into the unknown. Take it anyway. It's worth it.

The way I respond when someone walks into my environment, instantly sends a message about how I feel about them. Do I give them my attention? Is it my full attention? Do I smile? Do I get up and hug them?

Or am I so busy on my phone, or my computer, or with a magazine, or watching television...that I barely acknowledge their presence.

It all sends a message.

What messages am I sending?

Ahas!

I'm important. A smile, an invention, a positive word of encouragement, the release of a creative spark of genius, a random act of kindness, a hug... they can all change a life. Forever. It happens every day and I have the potential to be a part of it.

I'm not that important. A hundred years from now my life will be a distant memory. A thousand years from now it will be as if I was never here. Cemeteries are filled with people who thought they were "Essential and Irreplaceable." They proved to be non-essential and completely replaceable in the grand scheme of things.

Somewhere in between these two realities is the balance point which guides my actions. That which inspires me to live to my full potential, and yet not be consumed by a false sense of ego.

Ahas!

Remember to live in the now, too.

It feels easy to get caught in the trap of doing things just because of what they may mean in the future. Working toward the next promotion, higher profile client, more global project, bigger house, nicer car…. All of which is fine.

If that's what I really want.

The truth is though, a dance class can be loads of fun, even if I don't plan on being a professional dancer. The same goes for playing sports, learning to cook, throwing leaves at someone, reading a book, laughing, and a thousand other activities.

Life is an aggregate of "right now" moments. If I'm always looking ahead, I miss out on the joy right in front of my face.

Ahas!

If I'm struggling with this, I should spend more time in the presence of young children. They are masters at it.

Ahas!

The more I judge myself, the more I find myself being judgmental of others too. But when I allow myself to be me, I so easily allow others to be themselves too.

❝*If you don't like your classes on a Monday morning, you'll probably hate your job on Monday mornings after you graduate. And there will be a whole lot more of those."*

I did an interview today. It was for a college radio station. The interviewer asked me to sum up my thoughts on life into just a few sentences. Something simple and applicable to their college student listeners.

That quote is what I came up with. I think it hits the mark. If students are going to invest all that time, energy, and money to go to college, they might as well learn about things they're interested in. Then they can put that knowledge to use and get a job they're interested in too.

I closed the interview by explaining, "Someone is making a living doing your dream job. It might as well be you." That doesn't just apply to college students. It applies to all of us.

Ahas!

Row row row your boat, gently down the stream. Merrily, merrily, merrily, merrily, life is but a dream.

In a moment of tired frustration and discontent, I suddenly thought of that nursery rhyme. What brilliant and comforting wisdom.

Ahas!

My environment is not the only determining factor in who I become. At the same time, if I want to be a chef, it's probably more likely to happen if I start hanging out in kitchens.

People are already having the adventures I want to have. They are experiencing what I want to experience. Learning the things I want to learn.

The more time I spend with people living the life I want to live, the greater chance I'll get to live it too.

Ahas!

When I stopped trying to figure out why everyone was so screwed up and just realized we are all different...it got easier. Then I could just go hang out with people who were different from me and not feel the need to judge, or try and be accepted.

Ahas!

The currency of success is not money. It's minutes. What percentage of my life do I spend doing what I want, in the way I want?

That's true success.

Ahas!

It appears that the key to having a better relationship, more love, and a great sex life is quite simple. All I have to do is put a tiny filter between my thoughts and my words.

Before I speak, I think to myself—Is that a first date question? Or a first date comment? Or a first date tone of voice…?

If not, then I adjust until it is.

Ahas!

If it's not fun, I'm not doing it right.

This can be applied to pretty much everything.

Not all people are nice. I used to think that deep inside, everyone was. And maybe at the deepest soul level that's still true. In human form though...not all people are nice.

That doesn't mean I should be afraid all the time. Or constantly worrying about what might happen because some people aren't nice.

It means if I'm around people who aren't nice, then with no guilt, regrets, or self-condemnation, it's OK to leave and go be around people who are nice.

Ahas!

If I'm going to let my past dictate my future, I should at least choose a positive part of my past.

Ahas!

It happened again today. I was in the midst of a personal pity party. Something had gone wrong. I was unhappy.

Then I turned and saw a small boy about six years old. He was in a wheelchair. He had no legs.

In that moment, I remembered how fortunate I am. My struggles are nothing compared to what he faces each day.

He is an angel. I am embarrassed that his soul has to play the part it does, in order to remind me to be grateful for what I have.

I challenge myself to live in a higher state of awareness.

Ahas!

When I stand amongst giant trees, I get the overriding sensation of the folly of so much of the human experience. We rush around like ants. Scurrying and running with this sense of self-importance. But the trees are quiet sentinels to the truth somehow. They know there's a bigger game at play. A larger purpose to it all.

If I stop scurrying around so much and just listen. Just be. I will begin to understand this other wisdom which the trees know completely.

Ahas!

Waiting until we're sick to start living a healthy life seems pretty ineffective.

Ahas!

Every expert started off knowing nothing about what they became an expert in.

I will not let what I don't know, keep me from what I can know. I will not let what I don't do, keep me from what I might do.

Ahas!

*T*rying to cover up my dissatisfaction just leads to more dissatisfaction.

I remember when my solution to spending fifty hours a week at a job I didn't like, was to race out the door every Friday and head straight to happy hour.

Three vodka drinks later, I didn't care how much I disliked my job. I didn't care about anything. But this wasn't a real solution. It was an attempt to conceal the pain, not get rid of it. And it just led to other problems. Like nasty hangovers and an aching body every Saturday.

When I am courageous enough to ask—what is the source of the discomfort or pain? And to keep asking until I get the real answer…then I give myself the chance for a real solution.

Ahas!

When I am courageous enough to seek out better alternatives. Ones that bring joy, contentment, satisfaction...instead of pain, then I give myself the chance for a real life.

Masking or hiding from the pain is not the courageous act. Rather the contrary. That is when I am most cowardly.

Ahas!

*T*he more new things I try, the less afraid I am to try new things.

Ahas!

My view of my world is a reflection of how willing I am to see the rest of the world.

Someone cutting me off on the road, no longer has the same sense of magnitude when I know a billion people will go to bed hungry tonight. Many of them children.

The store being out of what I want to buy, is less deserving of an outburst, when I know in most third world countries, an entire family will make less in a month than I spend in a day.

This becomes even more true when I have actually witnessed these realities of the world firsthand.

Ahas!

I am amazed at the way my creativity skyrockets when I spend time in nature. An hour walking in the woods, or exploring tidal pools by the ocean, and I come up with more ideas and solutions than when I sit at my desk for a month.

When I'm exploring, I'm in the mindset of an adventurer. Charting new paths, exploring the unknown, making new discoveries....

Which is what creativity is.

I used to think things had to be complex in order to be effective. So I would seek out very complex solutions to my problems. Complex methods to achieve my endeavors.

Only then, they were so complex they confused and intimidated me. So I never used them.

There are simple solutions to most dilemmas. And simple methods to enable me to achieve most of my life's aims. I'm better off finding those, and putting them into action.

Ahas!

The more I travel, the more I realize how completely unlikely it is that where I was born, is where I am best suited to live.

That place I was born is a single point on the planet, with a particular culture and feel. There are thousands of other points, each with their own culture and feel. When I am open to it, I can see those other options.

When I am courageous enough, I can make those options my reality.

Ahas!

With almost no words, the first ten minutes of the movie Up, says more than most movies do in their entirety.

Ahas!

I have found it to be of immense value to ask why I believe things. So many times I have no basis for a belief other than someone else told me it was true. Often when I was just a child.

And yet, I allow that single data point to direct the way I live my life and the thoughts I think.

Until I allow myself to challenge the belief.

To be authentically me, and in all honesty, to be happy, requires deconstructing my beliefs and only keeping the ones I know to be true.

Ahas!

Children seem to naturally understand that the path to success means moving past failure. A baby keeps trying to turn over, then crawl, then stand, then walk, despite countless failed attempts.

At times in my life, I have lost this spirit. I have forgotten to keep trying. I become afraid of what might happen if I fail.

But that in itself is the actual path to failure. Only when I keep trying, can I succeed.

Ahas!

Today I sat and watched animals in a zoo. When placed in a small cage, they either become lethargic and barely move, or they go crazy and endlessly pace back and forth.

What drives these behaviors is their lack of freedom. It kills their spirit, or drives them insane. An endless loop of behavior and thought.

As I sat there, I realized it is the same for us humans. Only we are often the creator of the cage we're in. We made it, then put ourselves in it, and then we stay there. Even though the exit door is permanently open.

Ahas!

I didn't pick where I was born or who I was born to. I do pick where I stay and who I choose to stay around.

Ahas!

It's amazing how energy works. I saw a great inspirational movie three days ago. I'm still thinking about it. I know from experience that the ripple effect of a movie like that will positively impact my mood, my state, my thinking patterns...for an entire week or more.

Today I wondered what my life would be like if I applied that realization to the energy I allow around me each day? What if I read just one inspirational story on the internet each day? View one inspirational video on YouTube each night? Watch one inspirational movie each week?

And in turn, I disconnect from the energy sources which negatively effect my mood.

Would those simple adjustments be enough to change my whole life? I think so. I'm going to try it and find out.

Ahas!

The world is full of beautiful places. If I don't like where I am, I should find someplace new. If I don't know how to live someplace new, then I should travel to new places first. It will open my mind to what is possible.

Soon the unknown will become known. The new will become familiar.

Ahas!

I am most free when I pick my activities and pick my roles. A woman should not be the cook or cleaner in a house simply because she is a woman. A man should not be a builder of things simply because he is a man.

If I like to cook, then I should cook. If I like to build, then I should build. Regardless of the roles others have played before me.

Ahas!

"*Everybody is a genius. But if you judge a fish by its ability to climb a tree, it will live its whole life believing that it is stupid.*"

- Albert Einstein

How I wish I had seen this quote and understood what it meant when I was younger. But better now than not at all. When I feel like I'm unhappily out of my element, I'm going to remind myself that in that moment, maybe I'm a fish trying to climb a tree.

Ahas!

When life seems to have lost its glow, it's often because I have become the someone that others want me to be, and not the someone I want to be.

That glow can easily be re-gained. All that's required is to go back to my Big Five for Life and my Purpose for Existing, and realign my life with those.

I have tried other behaviors. Like blocking out the feelings the lack of glow brings. Either by denial or dulling. It just makes things worse in the long run. Much worse.

Ahas!

It's amazing and sad how many unhappy parents try to get their very happy children, to join the unhappiness.

Ahas!

One of my recurring challenges has been getting so focused on the future that I miss out on the fun, joy, adventures, and all the rest of the great things right in front of me.

Then years later when I reflect on those times, I think—"I wish I would have been more present back then. Spent more time enjoying those moments instead of always pushing for some future victory, or worrying about some potential future problem."

Today I will enjoy today. Tomorrow will get here on its own. It always has. It always will.

Ahas!

When I let fears of failure keep me from living the life I want, I don't end up safe. I end up having failed.

Ahas!

*W*alking around a good science museum inspires me on so many levels. They are full of things I know nothing about. Fascinating things.

Crystals that form into beautiful, perfect shapes all on their own. Creatures with behaviors so bizarre they seem like something in a science fiction movie. Images showing planets, moons and stars in numbers so great my mind can't really comprehend them....

All of that and a thousand other examples are sitting there waiting to inspire me.

What an amazing planet we live on. There is so much to explore, see, and learn about. All I have to do is open my mind and go take a peek.

Ahas!

One of the greatest things in life is to walk around barefoot for a while. It gives me the chance to experience the textures of life through my feet.

I feel grounded when I do it. Connected in a way I can't really explain. Indoors, outdoors...it doesn't matter. A mix of the two...even better.

I remember growing up, we all wore our shoes outdoors and indoors. That was "normal". Then when I traveled in Asia, it was impolite to wear shoes indoors. Even in public places like a museum you'd go barefoot. That was their normal.

Life is about picking my normal.

And about going barefoot.

Ahas!

Life doesn't happen by chance. It happens by choice.

I am the chooser.

Ahas!

Instead of wishing my life was more like someone else's, I should learn what they did to have their life, and create my version of it.

This requires a level of self-confidence I didn't have when I was younger. Back then I would see someone else's success and judge it. Find ways why it was unfair. Justify why I didn't have it or couldn't have it, or didn't need it.

I would create stories in my mind and tell them so often that I believed them. "Those people didn't have to work as hard as I did. They had it easier than me. It was all handed to them. They were born prettier, more handsome, taller, smarter, a different color…."

While some of it may have had elements of truth, a far bigger truth is that those judgements were my inner demons and they weren't serving me well.

I am capable of anything. I can be anyone.

Ahas!

When we look up at the sky on a starry night, what we can see is less than .00000005% of the stars in our galaxy. That is just our galaxy. There are at least one hundred and twenty-five billion more galaxies out there.

If a guiding presence can create all of that, surely the manifestation of my dreams are well within its capabilities. It is up to me to ask for guidance, and honor what I receive by acting upon it."

Ahas!

I don't have to have all the answers. A lot of curiosity and a willingness to ask all kinds of questions will take me far.

Ahas!

My unconscious is always sharing clues for how I can live an amazing life. I just have to remember to use the mute button appropriately.

Sometimes it's getting myself off of mute. Remembering to open the line of communication with my unconscious. To connect to my inner voice. Feel my instinctual guidance.

Other times it's muting all the craziness and noise around me so I can even hear my unconscious.

Ahas!

The small things are often overlooked. But the truth is, it's the small things which really matter. When I think of my favorite memories as a child, they revolve around a particular toy I loved, or something small my parents did, or little adventures I would go on.

There is so much cultural pressure about the Big things for kids. Getting them into the right programs. The right schools. Access to the latest and greatest technology. And it seems like that pressure is starting when the kids are younger and younger.

I think if those Big things are gotten at the expense of the small things, like being there for your kid's kindergarten costumer party, a lot has been lost.

Alas!

Both the parent and child miss out on the opportunities which create the most genuine smiles, the most lasting memories. And probably have the most significant impact down the line.

Ahas!

When I'm not sure what I want to do in life, I should stop doing the things I don't want to do.

Even if it's for just five minutes a day at the start.

The creation of that open space allows good things to grow and evolve.

My life today is a reflection of my choices today. If I want a different life, I must make different choices.

At times this feels hard. I'm afraid to make different choices because I don't know what they will bring. My fear of the unknown is greater than the pain I associate with my current situation.

But when I project myself forward. Five weeks, ten months, twenty years.... And with an honest heart look at what those futures will be if I don't make different choices...I find my courage.

Ahas!

Living my life's purpose doesn't mean I have to be pushing furiously forward every minute.

Life is a series of ebbs and flows. Pauses and quiet are part of the experience. No matter how on purpose I am.

How I define myself becomes what I am willing to accept in life.

I met a man recently who defined himself as "an angry guy." He said he wanted to be nicer to his wife and children, but he was just "an angry guy." Twice a week, or more, he yelled at them uncontrollably. Doors slamming, people crying....

I couldn't help but think that by applying the "angry guy" label to himself, he justified his behavior. He created a self-fulfilling, and self-allowing prophecy. Had he defined himself as "The Best Dad in the World" or "The Nicest Husband Ever," would he still accept the uncontrollable yelling, door slamming and people crying?

Ahas!

We all do this in different ways, I guess. Define ourselves. "I'm fat, I'm shy, I'm poor, I'm stupid, I'm a failure...." Those are all options. Defining myself in those ways will lead me down certain paths.

On the other hand, so will, "I'm adventurous, I'm loving, I'm smart, I'm an athlete, I'm successful...."

Since I get to choose, I will define myself by those instead.

Ahas!

If I'm not careful, I can get so caught up in what is going on in other people's lives, that I forget I have one of my own to live.

Ahas!

The more I believe in my own self-worth, the more I inspire others to believe in theirs. That's how I change the world.

Ahas!

I took my four year old daughter to a theme park today. After an hour of wandering, we decided to take a little break and enjoy a snack at an outdoor patio area.

Music was playing, people were smiling and wandering around. It was very festive. To our left was a giant lagoon all decked out with foliage and flowers.

In the mist of this pleasantry, up wanders two wild ducks to the table where we were sitting. My daughter was very excited because they literally walked right up to our table, walked around for a while, and then wandered away. A great chance for her to see them up close.

Then I noticed something that made me go hmmm. As the ducks wandered away from our table, and up to the next table, the guy sitting there became very agitated.

He was sitting and eating, and he literally took the time to move his arms and feet at the duck, in what

Ahas!

appeared to be somewhat of a territorial display. This attempt to shoo them away went on for many minutes.

And I found it odd. I struggled to comprehend the big threat. Had I missed something? Was there a more significant danger here than I realized?

Sure they were wild ducks, which meant anything was possible. Although to be fair, I haven't seen too many Discovery Channel episodes of wild mallards going for the jugular and taking down a human—especially at an amusement park.

I guess they could have pecked his feet, but the guy was wearing gym shoes, not the potentially peck hazardous flip-flops. Was it concerns over an ankle nip perhaps? A childhood incident gone wrong where a kindly offered piece of bread resulted in lifetime duck trauma? Bird flu worries?

After all, if Steve Irwin the crocodile hunter could get taken down in a freak stingray accident, isn't anything possible? Of course, this was a duck, not a stingray.

Ahas!

The answer escaped me. It still does. What didn't escape me though, was the bigger messages this duck encounter brought me.

Life throws lots of "ducks" at us. Some are real ducks. Some are annoying people. Some are opportunities outside our area of interest. Some are cool things we're actually interested in. Others are tweets, texts, emails, junk mail, news headlines, people's comments...and a broad assortment of other "ducks".

And when they come at us, we've got a choice. We can give them a quick look and if we like them, give them more time. If we don't, then don't.

OR, we can allow ourselves to get all distracted by the ones we don't like. Waving our feet and hands and taking up lots of time and mental energy.

It seems like the most content people I know, choose the first option.

And the most unhappy people choose the second. Then they complain they don't have enough time to do things they really want.

That person at the theme park gave me a great gift. He reminded me to be observant of my actions. And avoid wasting my time and energy shooing away non life-threatening "ducks".

Question: "What surprises you most?"

Dalai Lama: "Man. He sacrifices his health in order to make money. Then he sacrifices money to recuperate his health. And then he is so anxious about the future that he does not enjoy the present. The result being that he does not live in the present or the future. He lives as if he is never going to die. And then he dies having never really lived."

I think about this quote often. Its simplicity centers me somehow. Pulls me back from the minutia of the day-to-day in life. Takes me to a place where I view my existence with a much broader perspective.

If the actions, perspectives, and approaches of the people around me don't inspire me to new heights, it's time to be around new people.

If nobody wants to be around me, maybe I need to look at my actions, perspectives, and approaches.

Ahas!

Some days all things seem like big things. Then you hear of a friend who has been diagnosed with a serious illness and nothing seems big.

It's all perspective.

Ahas!

So much of what I have access to has been granted to me simply because of the country in which I was born. I did nothing to earn those privileges. And others who were born elsewhere did nothing to make them unworthy of those privileges. Yet I have been given them and those others have not.

These thoughts humble me. They remind me to be grateful. To be gracious too.

Ahas!

*T he more time I spend looking at the car crash,
the greater chance I will become the car crash.*

The applications of this are infinite.

Ahas!

It's amazing how having something to look forward to changes my energy. Even something as simple as recording and watching a favorite TV show makes me look forward to that day of the week in a different way.

So what if every day of the week I had one thing like that? Play volleyball one day. Go fishing one day. Favorite TV show one day. Write one day.... Even if it was just one hour on each of those days, it would give me something so fun to look forward to.

I'm going to do that. I'm going to make sure I have a standing appointment for at least one hour per day, every day, for something I genuinely look forward to. And I'm never going to schedule over those appointments with "more important" things. They will be my most important things.

Ahas!

Some days I feel like I don't want to get out of bed. I bet this will change that.

Ahas!

What would the "me" from thirty years in the future, tell the me that is alive right now?

Ahas!

When something has happened which is different than I expected, and not in a good way, my initial reaction is frustration, anger, disappointment.... But that's pointless.

There is no value in lamenting the situation, or allowing my mind to create drama around it. Who is to blame? Why me? This isn't fair!!!

Those are my first reactions. All are pointless though. The event has happened. It is my new reality. The only useful course of action is to figure out what to do now and start doing it.

An exception to this being only, perhaps, giving myself enough time to reflect on what has happened to figure out my role in creating the situation. So if I don't want it to happen again, I understand the way to avoid that path in the future.

Ahas!

The goal of my life is not to "make it through the day." It's to enjoy the day. Having this new perspective has changed so much for me. In a positive way, it challenges me to look at my decisions, my activities, my choices…in very different ways.

Ahas!

I've been trying a little experiment lately. Controlling time. The results have been pretty interesting. When I'm late for something, instead of constantly looking at the time, I focus on doing the best I can to move forward. And I keep a positive attitude about the situation. I keep my breathing nice and calm, and tell myself, "Everything will be fine."

Looking at the time every few seconds, which is what I used to do, has no value. It just makes me frustrated. With each minute that passes, I become more irritated.

Ever since adopting my new approach, good things have happened. Most of the time I end up arriving on time, even though it seems impossible. The other times I arrive later than I wanted to, but when I get to where I'm going, something has happened to make me not late.

The event has been delayed, the other person isn't there yet….

Plus, with my new approach, when I arrive, I'm not flustered or worried. I'm calm.

Ahas!

I don't know why this works. And I have to be doing my part too. I can't wait to leave until five minutes before I'm supposed to be somewhere, and it's a forty minute drive to get there. I have to be doing my role in getting to my destination on time.

When I do that though, and use this new approach, it feels like I control time somehow.

Ahas!

Great experiences taste sweet each time we think about them. Dreams left unfulfilled become more and more bitter.

Ahas!

A dying plant springs back to life with a little nourishment. We're just like the plant. The nourishment is a sense of purpose.

When I have that, I approach my whole life differently. No longer am I a stick, being tossed and thrown in the raging waters of the river. Being carried downstream at the whim of sources other than my own.

Instead, I become the captain of my ship. I have freedom. I am able to align all my resources towards the ports of call where I want to go. My life has purpose, direction, intensity, passion.

Why am I here? I will ask that question until I know the answer. Because that answer, is my purpose in this life.

Ahas!

My current reality is not the key determinant of my future reality. If "this" isn't working, I can change it.

There are millions of realities out there. When I stop for just a moment, and get out of my reality long enough to really look at the world around me, I can see them.

I am the one who gets to choose which of those will be mine.

Ahas!

When I commit to a path aligned with my purpose, the wall of turbulence formerly in my way, realigns to become the driving force which carries me forward.

The speed and strength of the realignment is in direct proportion to the clarity and intensity of my thoughts and actions.

I must commit. I must draw the line in the sand and say, "This is where I'm going. This is when I'm leaving." I must take action. Saying I want to go, is not the same as starting to walk.

And I must be adamant that nothing will keep me from what I seek. Adamant in my thoughts. Adamant in my actions. Adamant in all things.

Without that, the universe, or God, or whatever force is acting in cohort with us in this great adventure, does not know how to help me. Neither does anyone else.

Ahas!

When one minute I am walking north, the next south, the next east, and the next I am standing still.... And the whole time I am unsure of all of them.... How could anyone know how to help when that is my behavior?

Ahas!

*T*he value of good advice, is directly proportional to the degree to which I put that advice into action.

Ahas!

The great fear is not that we will die. It is that we will get to the end of our life and realize we have not lived.

That will not be me. I will have lived the life of my dreams. The question is not—Who am I to...? The question is—Who am I not to?

About the Author

Following a life changing event when he was thirty-three years old, John was inspired to sit down and tell the story of his first book—The Why Café. He had no previous experience or academic training as a writer.

Within a year after its release, word of mouth support from readers had spread the book across the globe—inspiring people on every continent, including Antarctica. It went on to become a #1 Best Seller, and has been translated into more than twenty-five languages.

John has since written other books, including Life Safari, The Big Five for Life, Return to The Why Café, and now Ahas!. He coauthored the book How to be Rich and Happy.

Through his writings and appearances on television and radio, John's simple yet thought provoking messages *have inspired millions to live life on their terms. In response to his endeavors, he has been honored alongside Oprah Winfrey, Wayne Dyer, and Deepak Chopra as one of the one hundred most inspirational thought leaders in the field of leadership and personal development. All of this continues to humble and amaze him.*

When he isn't writing, he is often out traveling the world with his family.

To learn more about John, please visit;

www.johnpstrelecky.com

Ahas!

My Aha! Moments

Ahas!

Ahas!

Ahas!

¡Ahas!

Ahas!

Ahas!

Ahas!

¡Ahas!

Ahas!